The Unlikely Entrepreneur

Robyn Johnson

The Unlikely Entrepreneur

How I Transformed $100 Into A Seven Figure Business

By

Robyn Johnson

I must create a system
or be enslaved by another man's;
I will not reason and compare:
my business is to create.

-William Blake
"The Marriage of Heaven and Hell"

CONTENTS

ACKNOWLEDGEMENTS

To my husband, Nate, my partner, my center, my joy,
and my home.

My children, Elias and Celina,

May you always find the courage to take chances in your life.
May you fail and get back up enough times to reach your dreams.
May you always know how deeply you are loved by us and by
God and that you are surrounded by people who see you as the
extraordinary people that you are.

CHAPTER ONE:
THE UNLIKELY ENTREPRENUER

I am not your typical entrepreneur. I never had a lemonade stand growing up or even sold Girl Scout cookies. Before starting my business, I was in about the least capitalistic profession possible—I worked for a church. I planned retreats, prepared children for Sacraments, and regularly made a complete fool of myself to earn the trust of the young people I worked with.

We didn't start this business with a large, official business loan. I took $100 from our emergency fund, which was more than a lot of money to us then. My start was not glamorous. I woke my 3-year-old son and infant daughter every Thursday, Friday, Saturday, and Sunday mornings to go from one garage sale to another to find items and resell them on Craigslist. Then I would go into work at the church.

From selling on Craigslist, we moved to eBay, Amazon, our

own website, coaching, consulting, web design, and creating courses. We have sold over a million dollars' worth of products on Amazon and hundreds of thousands of dollars' worth on eBay. I have also taught courses to eager students who have used my methods with success on a worldwide scale.

I also don't possess the typical credentials associated with running a successful business. I don't have an MBA; I don't even have a Bachelor's degree. I was a mom with two young children who built her business from nothing. I created the living and the life that I know share with my husband, our employees, contractors, and partners.

My motivation for writing this book comes from my desire to share my success with others. I want to empower other individuals to take the jump and find their own success story. If you have the courage to take a risk and the fortitude to do the work, you can have success. I have seen this exact scenario play out in my family. For example, my aunt, uncle, cousin, sister, and step-mom have all started successful online businesses. They ranged from an immigrant from China, teachers, and servers, and they were all able to make money selling online. Additionally, many individuals whom I have coached have started with nothing, only to build their unique success story. I want you to know before beginning this book that this is not just my story, it is real-life advice that is practical and easy to implement for anyone.

Who Benefits From Reading This Book?
This book is for anyone who is hesitant, fearful, or frustrated when it comes to finding success in their lives. It is for the

person who is tired of being promised the moon only to get hard cheese. In other words, someone who is tired of not getting real results. If this scenario sounds familiar, this book is written with you in mind.

If you are tired of pouring your energy, emotions, and money into one empty, fruitless program after another only to achieve the same lackluster results, this book is for you. If you have always wanted to have your own business but have no idea where to begin, this book is for you. If you are overwhelmed by the vast options available and are confused by contradictory advice, this book is for you.

This book is for you if you are determined to succeed for yourself or for your family. This book will show you how to achieve freedom—freedom from having to punch in and out of a job you hate and freedom to be your own boss, make your own decisions, and set your own schedule.

In the past, I worked at a job I loved, really loved. I worked within my own community, mentoring and leading our youth to follow Christ's path. I loved my work, but let me tell you, what I love even more is to be held accountable only to myself. The only boss I answer to now looks back at me in the mirror each morning.

This book isn't fluffy, shiny, or sexy, and it most certainly doesn't contain the exclusive "Secret to Success." What I am offering is an organized, systemized plan to get you closer to financial freedom.

Since most of my core business is related to e-Commerce,

be it selling on Amazon, eBay, etc., much of the advice given in this book will apply directly to those following a similar path.

However, after starting several business, I have found these same principals hold true for most businesses. That said, different industries will have different standards for return on investment and the time to profitability. You can take the core advice in this book and apply it to any business.

What Are Streams of Income?

Currently in my business we earn money in several ways. Each business is a separate stream of income—meaning that each business is independent of the others and provides steady income to pay our personal and business expenses. Each business profits us more than it costs us, and we carefully track the costs of each business

We have our business selling on Amazon, which does very well. However, we are at the mercy of Amazon allowing us to sell on their platform, and they have the right to change the fee structures or what we sell at any time. What started me on this path to systemized processes, cash flow spreadsheets, checklists, and sticky note boards was the monster under my bed, Amazon.

I am a rule follower. You will meet few people that match me for my level of rule following. I have been known to buckle both kids in their car seats to move my car just ten feet. I diligently follow Amazon's rules, but I was still fearful at every turn of the threat of suspension, a policy violation, or even the risk negative feedback. I wanted to break free from the constant stress and worry that our biggest source of income could crumble and fall, and I did.

We also sell on eBay, where we also do well and earn a steady income that could support our family if needed. However, eBay has some of the same pitfalls as Amazon. We are really at the mercy of the marketplace (eBay). So to a degree, we don't have complete control over our own business.

Each business, or income stream, provides income that you can count on month after month. Income that you can grow. We have spent a lot of time developing multiple businesses, or streams of income, so that if, for example, something were to happen to me or if Amazon was to suspend our account, we would still be able to provide for ourselves and our employees.

Having a business with multiple streams of income is much like playing Jenga. You build the tower and remove each unnecessary piece or process. You want it to be balanced and have a strong foundation, which is why you never remove the bottom pieces. You want it to have strength and flexibility while also trimming the excess costs.

Each income stream is a business that is independent of your other sources of income or businesses. It provides stability and security as you grow. You will want to build one business (income stream) at a time so that you can have tangible success quickly.

Why What I Teach is Different

Like I said, this isn't sexy, you won't get rich quick, and you will definitely have to work more than 5 hours a week. There is no magical get-rich-quick secret, and there are no shortcuts. My method involves hard work, determination, and a lot of failure. That's right—you're going to fail, and you're going to get used to it. You will to turn your failures into a success story, because if you don't know what doesn't work how are you supposed to find what does? Not everything I do will make sense to you. I'm not selling my ideas; I'm teaching you how to problem solve your own unique business plan.

The glory of an entrepreneur is their independence and uniqueness, and I am not here to take that away. What I teach is inherently conservative. So, if you are a high-risk kind of person, you probably won't agree with the pathways I lay out and recommendations I make in this book. The way I will teach you to begin growing your capital is with a low barrier entry. The good thing about this method is that it means you only have to have a little bit of seed money to begin. There is no demand for a huge investment, so no worries if you don't have a lot of resources at your disposal.

One question I get asked often is if someone has more money to start their business, will that allow them to turn a profit quicker? I have coached a good number of people. I will tell you without a doubt in my mind—your attitude plays a much bigger role in your success than the capital you start with. In fact, I see almost the opposite of what you would expect. Sometimes those with the least capital do the best because they have the strongest desire to win.

I don't like to take risks and am pretty conservative financially. I don't care if you are starting out with $100 or $100,000, my method doesn't deviate. Start with small purchases over a variety of niches. Start in one marketplace and branch out from there. This isn't Vegas, we're not on vacation, and your family's income stream isn't something you are going to gamble. Go wide, not deep. We don't get married to our products. If they become un-profitable for you, drop them and move on. You don't try to make it work, no re-purposing, no re-packaging, no advertising or staying up all night worrying about your $5,000 of stale inventory. Go wide not deep.

Robyn Johnson

CHAPTER TWO:
SECRETS FOR SUCCESS

People love a good secret, and when the secret has to do with how they can become successful and make money, they want to hear this nugget of wisdom all the more. In fact, people are always asking me the secrets of my success. When I tell them the secret is hard work, that often results in even greater interest. They lean in more and get a bit closer as if maybe I will whisper the "real" secret quietly in a hushed tone, because, surely, I didn't really mean hard work is the secret. But, in truth, the real secret is often not what they want to hear. It isn't a magic pill or secret formula that you can do A, B, C and then realize unheralded riches. Nope. All my "secrets" involve hard work, determination, and a drive to succeed. But, they do work, so if you are willing to try, you will be able to use these three secrets to find your own pathway to success. So, without further ado, here are my three secrets to success...

Secret 1:
Work Hard, Then Work Harder Still

This secret is pretty self-explanatory. The secret to starting a business from nothing is by working harder than you have ever worked before. Work harder than you ever thought possible, and then working harder than that. It means sacrificing some things. You might have to give up your favorite TV show or even Facebook. Remember, if you are willing to make the sacrifices and put in the work, I can assure you the sacrifices will be worth making once you obtain success.

Secret 2:
Don't Quit

If you're putting money into something month after month and it isn't working, that doesn't mean it's time to quit. It means it's time to find a better solution, a solution that will work. One way to do this is to seek out mentors who are getting the results you want and emulate them. One of my friends, Nathan Bailey, frequently says, "Emulate before you innovate." I believe his advice to be intrinsically wise. After all, people who are successful have already figured something out. Why not learn what they have done and copy what applies to your pathway to success?

Secret 3:
Be Willing to Fail

The hugely successful author of the Harry Potter series, J.K. Rowling, once said the following about the benefits of failure:

"Failure is so important. We speak about success all the time, but it is the ability to use failure that often leads to the greatest success. I've met people who don't want to try for fear of failing."

The risk of failure is part of the process of success. For example, love is risky. Growing up I hadn't had the best view of marriage. As a child, I don't think I really knew more than two or three adults in my life with strong marriages. So love, especially the kind that leads to marriage, seemed very dangerous to me. When you fall in love, there is a good chance your heart will get broken. However, love is worth the risk of failure. I can tell you that personally taking the risk of loving my husband has been one of the best adventures I have ever had. There was a time I was tempted to push him away because I was afraid of falling in love, afraid I might get my heart broken. I am so glad that I did take that leap of faith, though. I leaped right into his arms and never looked back.

When I left my job to pursue this business full time, I felt that familiar fear. What if I fail? Everyone would know I gave up a great job for a foolish idea. What would it mean for our family financially? We didn't have a lot of room to make mistakes as things were still very tight. Was I really making the right decision? I did the numbers what seemed like a million times. I made the jump. Now I am so glad that I did. If I hadn't, I would have missed out on the amazing life I have now.

Finding success often means you take the risk even though you know failure is possible. Starting a business is risky, much like being in love. It's hard sometimes, and sometimes your friends will think you are crazy. I know the life I live right now was completely incomprehensible even just a few short years ago. But, because I was willing to fail, I found success.

Work hard, don't quit, and be willing to fail. These are my three secrets. Also, be willing to listen to other people who have found success and take their advice to heart. Those few things are what I have done that has led to my current success. Don't worry, this advice isn't all I have to say. Throughout the rest of the book, I will walk you through how to implement these secrets in your life and teach you much more in terms of business creation. Read on to learn the step-by-step process of building your business and creating your own steady streams of income.

CHAPTER THREE:
FOUNDATIONS

There are a couple of foundational skills and actions that have helped us grow our business as quickly as we have. From the time I met my husband, he has always felt very strongly about investing in each other. Early in our relationship, we spent a lot of time and money taking personal development classes, reading non-fiction books, and finding people in our lives that pushed us to be the best versions of ourselves. If you want to see some of the books that have impacted our lives and our business, we have those listed at www.BestFromTheNest.com.

One of the personal development courses we took that made a tremendous difference for us was the Curriculum for Living from Landmark Education. While Landmark's programs are not religious in nature, we found that it helped us with our spiritual journey. We also discovered that it helped us to communicate with more power, set goals, get out of our own way, and create a level of success that would have been impossible previously.

While our story is interesting, even more exciting is that this life and the results we have produced are available to you as well. It is possible for you to create a living. Having a way to make money is an expression of who you are, to have work is a joy, and to have a life is an adventure.

Start Here

If we were going to start all over again, this is what we would do:

Sell items in our home or take on a second job to get seed money to start. We have found that $100–500 is more than enough to start out. Our experience is that it is your attitude, not the amount of money you start with, that predicts success.

Anything of value was sold for capital in the beginning. We sold everything. One day, my son came up to me and asked, "Mommy, are you going to sell my bed?" There was nothing that was sacred, and he knew it. But no, we didn't sell my son's beloved Thomas the Tank Engine bed. We cut unnecessary bills like cable TV and pretty much all other luxuries. In fact, for a long time, we only turned on the TV for the occasional cartoon for my son.

Buying Time

For some people, they have money to start, but they just don't have any time. In that case, where we would start is by asking the questions,

- What can we outsource so we can buy time?
- Can we pay for a house cleaner?
- Can we have a virtual assistant complete a task from our regular job?
- Can we have somebody who takes care of the lawn mowing?

There are ways to buy time. You can buy time by paying others to do things in your life so you can spend that time on profitable action items for your business. If you outsource your accounting, the time you save by not doing the accounting yourself should be spent in a way that produces 2–3 times the cost of the accountant. You would take the 8 hours a month your accountant saves you and use that time to source items for resale or list items for sale.

Sometimes, you have to do something for a short time that isn't fun or isn't what you want to do in the long term. When

I first started this business, I was so excited about the money that we were making on Craigslist and eBay that I called one of my friends who had done businesses with us in the past. I was so excited to tell her about the wonderful success we had. After I had shared with her, there was this long, awkward pause in the middle of the conversation. She said, "I can't believe you're just selling out. This isn't who you are. You're not a person who just sells junk on the internet." I didn't have a way to convey to her that this was just a stepping stone.

"Selling junk" was just a temporary moment. We were going to be doing things short-term so that we'd have the capital that we needed to do what we wanted to do long-term. When we started buying and selling on Craigslist, I will tell you, it was not fun. It was dirty. It was exhausting. Starting a business is in a lot of ways similar to having a child. Your business will be a living thing that will require constant attention in the beginning. When you're starting a business, you want to ask,

- Is this the right time in your life to be starting something that is going to be very time-consuming?
- Do you have at least 4 hours a day to work full tilt on this to get it moving?

In order to make a business work, you have to want it bad enough to crawl through glass. What I mean by that is that you have to be willing to say, "Whatever it takes, I'm going to make this work." There's nothing wrong if this isn't the right time. You can still keep reading this book, and you can still keep looking at business ideas. You might be waiting for the right idea, and you might be waiting for the right time in your life.

In the third chapter of the book of Ecclesiastes, it is stated, "For everything there is a season and a time for every matter under heaven." Further in the passage it says, "A time to plant, and time to harvest." Even if you aren't a person who is religious or who comes from a Judeo Christian background, the advice given in this passage still holds truth. When you have young children, it might not be a good idea to start a new business. If you have ailing parents, now might not be the right time to create a business from the ground up and have a four- to six-hour a day commitment. If that's the case, there's nothing wrong with waiting for the right time.

Slow, Steady, Serve

If we had to start over, one thing I think we would do the same way would be to build our business slowly, over time.

Let's say e-Commerce went away for some reason. We would start looking for a new way to generate income that comes from being of service to other people. If you haven't read Rabbi Lapin's book *Business Secrets from the Bible: Spiritual Success Strategies for Financial Abundance*, I highly recommend it. It's all about looking at your business from the perspective of service.

The question you should be asking when thinking about starting a business is not, "How can I make the most money?" Rather, you should be asking, "How can I serve others in a way that provides value?" When you start from this mind frame, business opportunities are everywhere. We would start by asking, "What skills and what service can we offer that would provide value and be of service to our customers?"

Multiple Streams

Once we had mastered our first stream of income, we would start training people to handle that for us. We would add a new business that brought in consistent money for us. The reason multiple streams are important is because even if you have a traditional business, you always need a backup plan.

For example, in a brick and mortar clothing store, you're still going to have things that are going to impact your business that are out of your control. There could be construction on the road outside of your store. There could be a new law that affects your business. A lot of resellers doing toy and children's consignment went out of business when the US passed a law saying that even items for resale had to be lead-tested. There could be a new political environment or a recession.

It's always good to have multiple streams of income, whether you're selling in a marketplace or have your own store. Having multiple ways to bring in income provides a level of security you don't have if all of your eggs are in one basket.

Save for a Rainy Day

One thing that I wish we had done better from the beginning was to save. We became so focused on building our business early on that we didn't save enough. Luckily, we were always able to make it through. However, looking back, this is one thing I might have done differently.

Managing Cash Flow

In the beginning, I can't tell you how many nights I spent staring at my Amazon Payouts wondering if I was actually making any money.

Managing your cash flow allows you to have the capital you need to make good inventory purchases. It also makes sure you aren't having a lot of sales with little to no profit.

Overhead Cost—Determining your operating cost is the first step in the cash flow process, including everything from

- Subscriptions/Amazon Monthly Fee,

- Internet,

- Boxes, and

- Tape.

Once you determine how much it costs you to actually operate your business on a monthly basis, you want to make sure you are a least generating enough gross profits to cover your expenses. From there you can look at your cost and create buying goals that are directly associated with your margins.

For example, say you are working with products that have a 50% return on investment, and your business costs you $100 a month. If you sell $400, that is your gross sales. That is NOT your profit.

To determine your profit, you need to take out the cost of goods. So let's say you spent $200 on the items you sold.

$$\$400-\$200=\$200$$

However, you still have to pay $100 for Amazon fees and the cost of your boxes, tape, and listing software. So your real net profit is $100.

This is just an example; your numbers will be different based off of your business.

Debt

People always ask me about taking on debt. Our recommendation is to not take on debt, especially in the beginning. As shiny, attractive, and tempting as it may be, taking on debt when you are still in the early stages (first 1–3 years) of a business can be very dangerous.

Although it might sound like your speeding your business growth up by increasing your working capital, you are really only creating more strain on your operations. If you take out a business loan, you need to already know what inventory you are going to purchase with it.

When starting a business, you will make most of your mistakes at the beginning. The more money you have, the bigger the mistakes you can make. Debt repayment can also have a negative impact on your cash flow. Even if you invest that debt wisely, and you're seeing great returns, having to pay that money back at a quick rate can suck the wind right out of your sails. We have also seen that debt can generate much anxiety for some people—so much so that it paralyzes them.

For these reasons, we encourage you to take the time to think about whether taking on debt is right for you. We have taken on debt from time to time to help our business grow. However, looking back, I can see that the times we grew the best were the times that we let that growth happen organically, and we didn't try to rush things by taking on debt.

If you are committed to taking on some debt to be able to grow quicker, there are some recommendations that I have. The first is that you need to do the math. For example, in a lot of the online spaces, there are these loans with the payback in six months. If you borrow the money, you will need to invest it quickly into high margin, quick turning inventory. If not, you might have to pay back a portion before you have had time to turn over product, which means that you will want to have a cash reserve in the bank, especially for the first loan payment. You need to do the math to make sure that you're moving quickly, investing the money you borrowed as profitably as possible, and managing your inventory turn rate. You must manage your margins very, very well if you're going to take on debt.

Debt can be expensive. Any time you increase your expenses, you have to watch your profit margins even more closely to make sure that you're making the money that you think you are. The other thing that I would say about taking on debt is to only do it after you have enough data that you can see what's going on in your business. Your business should have been producing consistent results over time. You should be able to say, "If I were to increase the capital by X amount, I could expect Y as the result of taking on this debt." You want to be able to have been doing what you're doing long enough to be able to predict what you can expect your results to be. Plan for the worst-case scenario. What will happen if

- Something doesn't sell?
- Something gets stuck on a boat from China?
- Amazon changes the rules on an item, and you are unable to sell it on the platform you intended?

You need to know what your fallback strategies will be. That's going to keep you from getting yourself backed into a corner.

No Shortcuts

One mistake that I see a lot of people make in business is they look to try to take shortcuts. If you've ever watched the ABC show *Once Upon a Time*, Rumpelstiltskin has a phrase that I use quite often: "All magic comes with a price, Dearie." The only thing I can promise you about starting a new business is that there should be some hard work involved. There's no business in which you can just outsource everything immediately. There's going to be hard work required. Make sure you carefully consider the ramifications—that is, the pros and the cons that come with having somebody else take on a small or a large part of your business for you right out of the gate.

There's a difference between hiring a contractor or hiring an employee to do something for you. For example, having someone pack boxes to send to Amazon or maybe clean some items for you to resell can be an excellent way to grow your business. However, having an entire company do all of your shipping to Amazon or do all of your sourcing for inventory will mean you don't have the control to make sure that things are getting done to the standards that you need.

This can lead to suspended accounts if you don't have a *trusted* partner. There is a time and a place to use services that help take the load of your business; however, make sure you are using trusted companies with reputations you can verify. Also, make sure you are making the decision because it is was is best for the business, not what will make you look good in the eyes of others.

Don't skip steps when it comes to your business; invest in a solid foundation. There are some excellent books that will help you grow as a business owner and as a person. Make sure that you listen to advice from various people with multiple points of view, even if they have different political or world views. Even though you might not want to be their best friend, they can have some great information that you can take insights from and use in your business. Watch out for shiny objects or people who always have new ideas for you to start a new business. Build one business (income stream) at a time. Stay focused on things that work, things that have been proven, and things that make sense mathematically. Look for simple business models that others have had success with.

Play Full Out

We've heard it said that "If you don't play, you can't win." What most people do in life is they assume if you don't play, then you can't lose. I think subconsciously, we believe "If I don't try, then I don't have to risk failing. I don't want to lose that hope of having that business one day." If you don't give something your best effort, part of you knows that you can use that as the excuse for why it didn't work out.

Play full out. If you're going to do something, do it well. Do it with excellence, and do it with integrity. If you fail at it after giving it everything you have, then that's okay. There's nothing wrong with failure. Failing doesn't make you a failure; failure is letting fear rule your life and actions. Failing just means that you gave it all you had, and it didn't work out.

This is great news! This way, you know without a doubt that it wasn't the right idea for you. If it was the right idea for you, and you played full out, and it was the right time, then it would have happened. Since it didn't, you're going to look for something else. If you failed in the past, that is good. That means that you know what failure tastes like, and you'll be driven to work even harder in your next pursuit.

One caveat: This is not a license to ignore your spouse if he or she feels like you're making reckless financial decisions or if he or she tells you that he or she has a bad feeling about something. If you care about somebody enough to spend the rest of your life with him or her, you should listen if he or she says that it feels like something is not right. Your spouse has more perspective than you do; if your spouse says that he or she doesn't like someone you trust listen to him or her. Make sure that you have your partner in alignment with what you're doing. It's going to make you a stronger businessperson, and you're going to need your spouse's support when things get hard.

Make Your Work a Game

Vince Lombardi said, "Plan your work and work your plan." It's something that has been a cornerstone of our business. You need to have a game plan. Another sage sole, Mary Poppins, said, "To everything that must be done, there must be an element of fun." We try to do that at Robyn's Nest. What we do is we try to make everything a game. If you have ever played a game with little kids, you know that they sometimes change the rules in the middle of the game. That's completely okay. In fact, I encourage it. If you are creating or working on your business, and realize you're not having fun anymore, change the game so that you can have fun again.

Part of the fun of playing a game is keeping score. So, when you create your plan or game for your business, you want to make sure you have a way to tell if you are winning the game you are playing. One thing that is critical is to make sure you measure what is important to you. For example, if I'm looking at my Amazon business, and I'm looking to measure my gross sales, so I just stay focused on my gross sales and nothing else. But then, I could end up having high gross sales yet losing money overall because I'm not watching my profit margins and my expenses. It's important to make sure that you measure the results that are really important to you.

Have Your Word Matter

Integrity is the last item on this list. But it is something that is first in my heart. If you want to create powerful results in your business, you need to start keeping your promises not only to others but also to yourself. Most people are good at keeping their word when it comes to others. If you are not, that is something that you should work on before you start your business.

There is a trap for some people that say they want to start a business: They take some of the steps, but because they don't keep their promises to themselves, they get discouraged quickly. You should keep your word to yourself not because someone else will think less of you but because who you are is someone who honors his/her word. C.S.

Lewis said, "Integrity is doing the right thing even when no one is watching." Guard your relationship with your word and integrity with your life!

Integrity and success in business go hand in hand. If you are going to invest in one thing, make sure it is that your word is your bond. Your integrity should always be at the forefront of how you run your business day to day. There is a reason so many successful businesspeople value their integrity above so many other aspects of their businesses. Dave Ramsey, Gary Vaynerchuck, and Brian Tracey all are leaders in business and entrepreneurism and all say that integrity is a cornerstone of who they are and is important in business. This is not a coincidence. If you take only one thing from this book, I hope it is the very real relationship between your integrity and your results in business.

"A master in the art of living draws no sharp distinction between his work and his play, his labour and his leisure, his mind and his body, his education and his recreation. He hardly knows which is which. He simply pursues his vision of excellence through whatever he is doing and leaves others to determine whether he is working or playing. To himself he always seems to be doing both". – J Michener

CHAPTER FOUR:
THE FOUR MILESTONES

I have built these milestones to use as your guide to creating, scaling, or enhancing your business. These milestones have worked for me and others. Within each of the milestones, there are common plateaus that tend to trap people and hamper their progress. A plateau is defined by Webster's dictionary as a period when something does not increase or advance any further. A plateau in your progress can prove discouraging and damaging to your state of mind. Consequently, I plan on sharing with you how to move past these business plateaus.

There is no official handbook on how to be a successful entrepreneur. In most cases, you are left on your own to make your way in business. However, I aim to give you some guidance in the form of these milestones that will point you in the right direction. It is important to note that your ultimate success is still up to you. I can only give you the map; it's up to you to follow through and let it guide you to the fulfillment of your dreams.

These milestones will also give you the basics of business that take time and experience to learn. After all, if you are like me, the reason you got into business in the first place had little to do with the desire to run and operate a business. You probably don't have an MBA in business or understand complicated business concepts. In most cases, the impetus behind a new business was a great idea for a product. Or maybe a desire to sell things in an attempt to help make ends meet for your family or the discovery of a talent that you have that you might be able to offer as a service. Terms like margin, entities, and inventory turn rates might sound like a foreign language to you now. But, after you go through this book, you will understand these concepts and their necessity in a sustained successful business.

Stages are very important in business, and having a good understanding of these various stages is crucial. The business elements mentioned above won't matter much before you make your first $1,000 in sales. But, after that point, you probably want to look at these things. That is why we have laid out the milestones in a simple way, allowing you to focus on the right aspects of growing your business at the right time. Of course, not everyone will want or need to complete all four milestones. After all, if your goal is a conservative one of, say, an extra $5,000 a month to supplement a retirement income, then you can probably safely stop at milestone 2 and still fulfill your goal.

It is also important that you don't limit yourself to someone else's idea of success, even mine. Your business is meant to serve you and your customers, no one else. So, consider my milestones as suggestions, not the Gospel. My goal is simply to make sure you are building a business that fits your life and that can grow with you. After all, you will change, your goals will change, and your life situations will change—so should your business. The milestones I plan to share will help you create a business that does just that.

When I first started my business, my kids were very young. As a result, I wanted to be home with them. My desire was to be able to reach that goal. When they started school, their needs changed a bit, but I still wanted to be available to them. I wanted to be able to attend field trips with them, be able to stay home with them when they were sick, and not have to send them out to daycare during school holidays. So, my being present for them was still crucial. As they have grown, my daily physical presence has become less crucial. Now, my family's needs have changed. Recently, my amazing mother-in-law had a short series of health issues. As a result, she needs my husband's help more than before, and we are very grateful to be able to assist her. As a result, my husband is home now more than I am. His priorities are primarily to take care of his mom and our children along with helping me grow our business. Now, I am enjoying the freedom of travel. In five years or six months, that might change yet again. Thankfully, the principles I used to build my business have helped me create a business that will change with me.

That is the beauty of creating a business that is fluid and flexible. If you want to travel or retire within a few years, you want to create a business that will not depend on your presence. In other words, you will transfer the work of running the business from yourself to others. I sometimes see people building themselves a prison cell of a business. They don't want to have any help, so they are unable to take even a few days off each year. There is nothing wrong with that; it just wouldn't work for my family's lifestyle. You have to be smart about not only building your business initially but also looking ahead to the future.

About the Milestones:

Don't be surprised to see some repetitive concepts within each milestone. They repeat because as you go through the milestones, you will be reassessing your goals. You will also be changing your goals on a monthly basis. It is important to note that changing your goals is not failing. Think about it as a game, a game that you want to win. Sometimes you might have to change the rules to make sure you can win and still have fun. As you grow, you will get a clearer picture of where you want your business to be. It is okay if that picture changes over time. Remember, not everyone needs to hit all the milestones.

Take what you get from this book and apply it to your life. Consider this a resource. It's not the one and only way to success. After all, there are as many different paths to success as there are businesses. The milestones are one way to make your journey towards success easier. That is all. You will see in milestone 1 that the first step is getting started. It's about doing the work to prove to yourself that you are serious in regards to your goals. You are getting real. You are ready to start selling and are committed to making a profit. By the way, in case you didn't know, all businesses involve selling something. But, don't worry. Even if you don't consider yourself a salesperson, you can still succeed.

In milestone 1, you will see why getting to that first $1,000 in gross sales is a huge step. At the beginning of your journey, this number will seem as unattainable as a million dollars. But, as you will learn, if you take consistent actions over time, you can achieve that amount fairly quickly. Just keep moving forward and following the methods that have been proven to work.

Milestones 2 through 5 are all about scaling your business, creating systems and processes that you can teach to others, building that team, and finding important consultants who are going to offer the expertise you need and want. For example, after you are making $5,000 a month in gross sales, I highly recommend you in invest in an accountant. He or she will save you much more than they cost and will help you navigate the tumultuous world of taxes and the IRS. Milestones 2 through 5 also include how to add streams of income. As your business grows, it becomes more and more important for you to have multiple streams of income to support your employees and your contractors if something were to happen to your main source of income.

"I went to the woods because I wished to live deliberately, to front only the essential facts of life, and see if I could not learn what it had to teach, and not, when I came to die, discover that I had not lived. I did not wish to live what was not life, living is so dear; nor did I wish to practice resignation, unless it was quite necessary. I wanted to live deep and suck out all the marrow of life, to live so sturdily and Spartan-like as to put to rout all that was not life, to cut a broad swath and shave close, to drive life into a corner, and reduce it to its lowest terms."- Henry David Thoreau

CHAPTER FIVE:
MILESTONE 1

In some ways, the first milestone can be the hardest. Getting your first $1,000 in gross sales can be challenging, because you have to choose exactly where you should start. As I said before, there is no manual for how to start a business. There has been a lot written, but it is hard to tell whose advice you should follow. One thing I always remind people of is to embrace your inner weird. Find something that makes you unique, something that you love and gets you excited, and then find out how you can make money doing that.

If you are already past milestone 1, my recommendation is for you to not skip this section. I hope you find enough value to skim it at least, just to make sure that there are no foundational pieces that maybe you've missed.

In the beginning, it is very important that you stay focused on that first milestone of $1,000 in sales. Don't let yourself get overwhelmed in trying to build an entire online empire overnight. You want to focus on results that you can get right away and show yourself that this will work. You need to prove to yourself that you can do this, which you can. More importantly, you need to see if this is something you want to do. Are you ready to create a living, breathing business that will require a lot of attention in the beginning?

Step 1.
Pick a way to sell.

If you don't have a lot of money to start your business, we are going to focus on getting you that seed capital first. We will look at a couple of ways that you can start a business quickly, easily, and with little to no capital and risk. It might be something you do for a short time so that you can get to your long-term dream. One word of caution, don't get so married to your long-term game that you can't find the perspective of what you need to do to take your first step.

While short term you might be selling things on Craigslist, or Amazon, what we're looking for over the long term is to provide you the seed money for you to create a business that is completely yours. You might, like many of my fellow e-Commerce counterparts, find that selling in a marketplace like Amazon or eBay gives you all the freedom that you need. Once you have multiple businesses, you can reliably produce a set income for you and your family, and you can always reevaluate to see if you want to take on something new.

Now, if you have money, but no time, then we're going to be looking at how you can buy time. How do you buy time?

It is much easier than one would think—by outsourcing certain tasks to others, you can have time to focus on the most profitable activities in your life and your business. For example, if you get paid $15 or more per hour at your job, what might be better for you is to continue working at your job and to outsource other pieces of your business. You could have someone in the Philippines create your listings for you or help you enter receipts into QuickBooks or Xero. I know many people who contract with people abroad to help them find products for resale. The goal in outsourcing is to get as much mileage out of your business when you first start.

If you need extra income to start, I have two models for you to gather your seed money in the resources sections. You can sign up to for the free lessons at

www.BestrFromTheNest.Com/Unlikely-Resources

At the time of this printing, there are step-by-step instructions for getting your first $1,000 in sales on Craigslist and Amazon.com.

We have used and taught both of these methods with success. They are solid ways to start without having to go deeply into debt. Both models are simple enough to start but can be grown into very large enterprises.

You will have to register for the site. However, there will be no cost. If you have any trouble registering, please email excellence@robynsnest.co.

If you have a specific idea in mind or don't want to start out with the above-mentioned models, there are other options to get that initial seed money. You could get a second job delivering pizza, babysit, tutor, clean houses, mow lawns, fix computers, organize home offices, be a caretaker for the elderly, or pet sit. There's a million different opportunities. Just go onto Craigslist and look at the services that people are offering, and see if that's something that you could do. Find what skills you have through which you can provide value to others, and offer those things as services so that you can get enough capital to build your business over time.

Brainstorm things that you're good at to help discover where your specialty lies. When friends come to you with questions or looking for advice,

- What subject or subjects are their questions usually related to?
- On what topic do they consider you an expert?

Those are the areas where you want to look.

If you have money but lack time, I recommend my course on Hiring and Training Virtual Assistants. You can find out more about this course at

http://www.bestfromthenest.com/hiringvassalespage/

Step 2.
Open a separate bank account.

No matter how small you intend your business to be, it is very important that you have a separate bank account for your business. You can open an account that is under your social security number for now, but you do not want to comingle your business and personal funds. Often you can grow faster than you intend. If you don't start out with a separate account, it will be difficult and expensive for an accountant to go back after the fact to determine which items were personal spending and which were business spending.

The other reason I like people to have a separate bank account right out of the gate is that it gives you an idea how much you want to invest. Take the amount that you feel comfortable investing in your business and put that in your business account. Then work within that budget.

It is ideal if you do not take any money out of your business for the first three to six months. If you have ever invested in a brick and mortar store or franchise, you realize this is an incredibly short period. Most businesses don't expect to turn a profit in the first year. Starting a business with the methods we teach allows you to be profitable quicker, but the business still does need time to grow before it will be able to provide you with a steady income. Waiting to pull money out of the business will allow it to grow much faster, and you'll be able to take more profit in the long run. If nothing else, try to wait at least three months before you take money out of your business; you can grow much faster.

Step 3.
Make it official.
Now, don't do this part unless you're really serious. If you're just playing around with the idea, and there's nothing wrong

with that, then don't do this part. Owning a real business is hard, and it's not for everybody. Legally setting up a business takes some effort, and it's going to be a big waste of your time if you're not serious about it. There are a couple things that you will want to do to make your business official.

Because you're going to be a business, most likely, you're going to need to remit sales tax. Unless you live in a tax-free state, you will need to remit sales tax for items sold in your city and state. You want to register for a Resale License, sometimes called a Transaction Privilege Tax License (TPT), and you're going to want to pick a business entity.

A business entity is just the legal form of your business. You can Google information on the common types.
- Sole-Proprietor
- LLC
- S-Corp

Then, contact an accountant or lawyer to see what the right option is for you.

Many people start out as a sole proprietor until they are making a profit. Then, most accountants have said to me that they recommend an LLC with an S-Corp election, but again, talk to an accountant or lawyer to find out what's right for you. I am not licensed in any state to provide legal or financial advice. Call your state and download the correct forms to file to obtain a business license and register your business name.

I also recommend you take this time to get business

insurance—especially if you have any assets (a house, a car, etc.). Business insurance is worth every penny. If you can't afford it today, make it a high priority to get within the first month.

I am not an account or lawyer. Contact a licensed professional in your area for advice. I am not giving you business, financial, or legal advice but rather advising you to seek counsel.

When it comes to naming your business, name it something general. Your business is going to be constantly evolving. If your plan is to be selling yo-yos, instead of naming your company Robyn's Yo-Yos, what I would do is maybe name it something like Robyn's Enterprises or RMJ Limited— something that's very general. As you grow and obtain multiple streams of income, that name fits as you continue to evolve as a business.

Before you settle on a name, make sure you do a trademark search. If you try to name yourself something like "Robyn's Disney Store" or "Diet Coke Enterprises," which include trademarked words, you will end up having to change your name later. There is also the chance you could be sued for trademark infringement.

It can also be a good idea for you to check to make sure that the name that you pick is available with the state corporation commission so that you can register as a business.

I also usually check and see if that domain is available. If so,

I would go ahead and purchase it. Registering a domain cost very little and gives you options as you grow your business.

Step 4.
Open your selling account or list your services.

Go to the link in the starting guides in the resource section at www.BestrFromTheNest.Com. You would start working on creating listings and finding products for either Craigslist or Amazon or eBay. If you're going to start a service-based business, then make sure you get yourself listed in Angie's List and Yelp. Make sure you get your services also listed on Craigslist, and put up signs locally to advertise your business.

Step 5.
Plan your work and work your plan.

The first step in planning your work is to determine by what point you want to have this milestone completed. Here is an example of how we work backwards to create an action plan.

If I want to have my first milestone of $1,000 in gross sales achieved by 3 months from now or if I want to sell $1,000 in services within 3 months, by the end of the second month, I would like to have a least $700 in sales. By the end of the first month, I'd like to have at least $400 in sales. This would mean in 2 weeks from now, I would need to have $200 in sales. Then this week I need to work at having $100 in sales.

Date	Revenue Goal
3 months from today	$1,000.00
2 months from today	$700.00
1 month from today	$400.00
2 weeks from today	$200.00
1 week from today	$100.00

Remember to stay focused on providing excellent customer service and in having integrity in what you do.

Step 6.
Tell everyone.

This is not the FBI. You do not need to be a secret agent. Make sure that you tell everybody that you know that you're starting a business. Ask for them to support you by helping you to eliminate things in your life that might keep you from staying focused on your tasks. Most people need an external accountability system or people who are outside of themselves to stay focused on their goals, so make sure you are setting yourself up to win.

Summary

Completing the first milestone will probably not be graceful. It's going to be a lot of figuring things out and making mistakes along the way. Give yourself room to make mistakes. As you grow, start to brainstorm on where you'd like your business to go next. Before we start milestone 2, we're going to look at how we can make sure that your business is healthy as it grows. We will also look at how to help you scale it at a reasonable rate that allows for the maximum amount of profitability.

"I just want to leave you with this thought, that it's just been sort of a dress rehearsal and we're just getting started. So, if any of you start to rest on your laurels, I mean, just forget it."
– Walt Disney on the 10 year anniversary of Disneyland

CHAPTER SIX:
MILESTONE 2

For some reason, I find that many Amazon sellers and those starting a local service seem to get stuck right around the $5,000 a month mark. One of the reasons for this is because when you are selling less than $5,000 a month, mostly you are just focused on trying to get the sales. You're learning the very basics. You're learning how to make sure you have the right inventory, how to price your items, and how to manage your inventory.

In the beginning, you focus on basics. However, once you hit $5,000 a month, your business becomes a little bit more complicated. At this point, there are certain things that you need to do to allow your business to continue to scale.

Remember: The milestones are only one way to scale a

business; there are many other methods. This is just what I have seen work. Make sure that you are customizing the content in this book to fit the needs of your business.

You may ask: Why are we using gross numbers as a way to measure success? Gross numbers give no real indication if a business is healthy or even profitable. In fact, somebody could be grossing $100,000 a month and be losing money consistently.

The reason that we're using gross numbers is because it's a way that we can measure our business regardless of where and how you sell. Every business is going to have a different expected return. For example, if you're selling used books on Amazon, we expect your return on investment (ROI) to be higher than someone buying products wholesale. When someone buys a book for $1 and sells it for $20, their margins are much higher than someone buying wholesale and only getting a 50% return on investment for the inventory that they're purchasing.

Using gross numbers is a way to talk to a lot of people in a lot of different business models without having to understand the different levels of margins of his or her business. Another reason I am not using the profit for the milestones is because profit is often calculated incorrectly. I often see new sellers on Amazon saying that they know they must be making money because they just got a $5,000 payout. The payout, or the amount you receive from a customer is not your profit. We will talk more about making sure your business is profitable later in this chapter.

One pitfall is to compare yourself to others. If you find that you get depressed by looking at Facebook posts from others saying that they sold a large amount over a period of a month, remember that is a gross number. It is possible for someone to make more money in profit at milestone 2 than at milestone four if the person at milestone 4 is not watching his or her margin.

Also, every business owner has a different set of circumstances. They could've started with a different amount of capital. They could have more time to invest in their business, or they could have had another business already that provided them with labor that they were easily able to reallocate to this business. Don't compare yourself to others, because you don't know what their situation is, and the same thing goes in reverse. Don't look down on a seller just because they are selling less than you do. There is always something you can learn from others.

You want to make sure that as you grow your business, you grow it in a way that fits your life. Make sure you are clear on your priorities as you grow your business. If you want to travel, if you have young children, or if you are continuing to work another position, make sure that your growth is planned around those priorities.

Stay focused on one stream of income before starting a new business or stream of income. The exception is if you have maxed out that stream of income. An example would be if you started with Craigslist and you've now maxed out the amount of income that you can generate by buying things at garage sales and reselling them on Craigslist. Then you would start a new stream and go to milestone 1 and work to be consistently producing $5,000 a month with that new stream of income.

The difficulty at milestone 2 is that you have to push through to a new level of entrepreneurship. At this level, just selling isn't enough. You will need to take the time to learn some business basics and make sure that your business is set up correctly. You will have to start monitoring areas in your business and assessing what is generating profit. In milestone 1, you learned to sell. In milestone 2, you are learning how to be a business owner.

Once you are making over $5,000 a month, I strongly suggest that you consult with an accountant. At this level of income, you can get yourself in a lot of trouble in the area of taxes without a good attorney or accountant reviewing your business. You need to be setting money aside for income tax, report and remit sales tax, and make sure you have the right type of business entity. An accountant or bookkeeper will make sure that your books are up to date and that your tax returns will be easy to process at the end of the year. If you have a good accountant, he or she will save you much more than he or she will cost you.

As we move through the milestones, one thing I suggest is to start building the foundation for you to build a team of people. Some choose to hire employees, some find great contractors, and some use a combination of contractors and employees. Taking the time in this milestone to create efficient systems will make it easier for you to expand and help maximize your profits even if you don't hire any help.

If you have no wish to hire help or have a warehouse, then your goal should be to maximize every penny spent in your business. The more efficient you can make your business, the more you make per hour. As a solo-preneur, you can make very good money and keep your expenses low. You can still follow the principles I teach in this and the other milestones to make sure you are getting the most out of your business.

Step 1
Goal setting.

When we work with clients, one of the things that we do first is we figure out where that person wants to go. If you don't have a goal, you don't have something you're moving towards, and it's very easy to find yourself working very hard but not getting anywhere. One of the things that you can do to goal set is to imagine yourself two years from now.

- What specific results are your seeing?
- What are your gross numbers?
- How much are you profiting?
- How many people are on your team?
- What things are you no longer doing yourself?

Imagine as if you are in the future and have already achieved these goals. This is not a pie in the sky idea; you should be able to imagine yourself in the future having already achieved these goals—much like an athlete envisioning himself crossing the finish line.

Write down what specific goals you want to see. Make sure

you have concrete numbers, not feelings. To create a plan or a game for your business, you have to have a way to measure your results to see if you are moving in the right direction.

Now we are going to create a plan to get you from where you are today to the numbers you just created. Take the numbers you wrote down, and we will work backward.

Let's say you were going to look at the goal of having $20,000 a month in gross revenue one year from today.

- What results would you need to have six months from now to make that goal attainable?

- What results would you need to have 3 months from now to make that 6-month goal attainable?

- What results would you need to have 1 month from now to make that 3-month goal attainable?

- What results would you need to have this week to make that one-month goal attainable?

What we would end up with is a table like this:

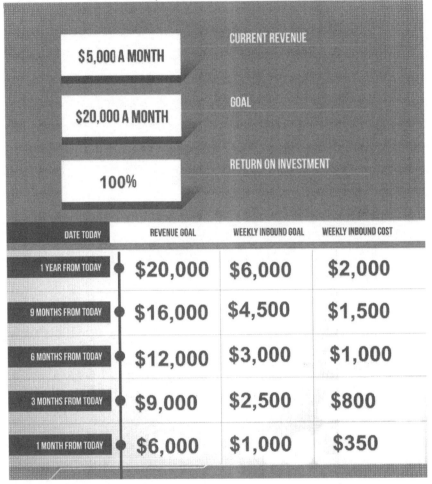

	CURRENT REVENUE
$5,000 A MONTH	
$20,000 A MONTH	GOAL
100%	RETURN ON INVESTMENT

DATE TODAY	REVENUE GOAL	WEEKLY INBOUND GOAL	WEEKLY INBOUND COST
1 YEAR FROM TODAY	$20,000	$6,000	$2,000
9 MONTHS FROM TODAY	$16,000	$4,500	$1,500
6 MONTHS FROM TODAY	$12,000	$3,000	$1,000
3 MONTHS FROM TODAY	$9,000	$2,500	$800
1 MONTH FROM TODAY	$6,000	$1,000	$350

These numbers are overly simplified and rounded to give you and example. I have more information on this table in the appendix.

From there, you can sketch out exactly what steps need to be taken for each week. What this does is it takes your goals and your ambitions out of that daydream, one day it might work out kind of feeling into an action plan that is attainable and realistic. Now you now have an actionable plan, find an accountability partner or coach and share the plan with him or her.

Make sure that you spend time developing your plan. Don't rush or skip this step. This step is very important. Even though you probably will be revisiting and changing your plan very often, having a good blueprint will get where you need to be. As you look at your plan, you will want to consider

- How you are going to scale your inventory,
- How you are processing your items for sale,
- How you are going to outsource your accounting or other duties, and
- What items you need to hire out first.

If you have a spouse or partner, they need to be involved in this conversation if they're willing, because this plan will affect them, and having their buy-in will help you meet your goals faster.

Step 2
Understanding your business.

It's not how much you make, it's how much you keep. Grossing a certain amount per month does not necessarily mean you have a healthy business. In fact, it is possible to gross $100,000 a month or more and be losing money. To make sure your business is healthy and growing at a reasonable rate, there're two things that you need to be watching. The first one is turn rate.

Turn rate is what you're going to look at to make sure that you don't have too much money held in inventory. Once you understand your turn rate, you can use the knowledge to understand how your inventory moves through your business. This understanding will make your business grow faster and more profitable. We'll talk about turn rate in more detail in the next milestone, but now we're going to focus on reducing stale inventory and also on using the metrics of your sales to make sure that you're only ordering and only sourcing enough inventory to cover you for the next one to two months.

The starting point for controlling your inventory is to see how long you are keeping your inventory. When you can reduce the amount of time you hold inventory, you increase the turn rate or the number of times that you can profit off of the capital you are investing.

As you grow, cash flow becomes very important. If all of your cash is tied up in inventory, you could end up unable to continue to cover your expenses.

Managing your inventory also ensures that what you are doing is working. If you are making good buying decisions for your inventory, then you should see you inventory moving at a steady rate. If you have stale inventory, it could mean that your items are priced too high or that you are purchasing inventory where there is not enough demand or too much competition.

So how do you determine if you have stale inventory? If you

are an Amazon seller, there is a report called the Amazon Inventory Health Report and it tells you exactly how many days you've had items in storage. We aim for around two months of coverage. Have you been holding things six months or a year or more? If so it might be time to

- Change the way you are buying inventory,
- Liquidate inventory to free up capital, and/or
- Adjust your prices.

If you had a brick and mortar store, you would look at your inventory on hand. If you didn't have dates of when you purchased the items, you could simply look for dust on the shelf. When you see you have inventory that isn't moving, that is when you would be marking down inventory for clearance and looking for ways to move that inventory faster.

Another way to move inventory, whether you are a brick and mortar store or selling on Amazon or eBay, is to look at another marketplace to move stale inventory. Find someone with a booth at a flea market, list items on Craigslist, and look for creative ways to move inventory that isn't selling through so you can focus on the profitable areas of your business. Sometimes it's better to cut your losses and move on than hold inventory indefinitely.

For inventory that is moving well, when we reorder we aim to carry only 4 to 8 weeks of stock at any one time. To do that, we look at how many items we sell per week and multiply that by the number of weeks we want to have inventory.

Now, some businesses are going to require that you hold stock longer. Some businesses have seasonal periods, so you would have to buy your stock more on speculation or the previous year's sales. Every business is different.

For this book, we're going to be focusing on a weeks of coverage range for 4 to 8 weeks. To determine what your weeks of coverage is for your inventory, you will need to know the quantity of the items that you have available. If you had 50 blue widgets, and you sell on average 10 a week, you would divide the total number of 50 by 10, and you would see that you have 5 weeks of coverage. When you order again, you want to make sure that you order between 6 and 8 weeks of stock. Your next order of blue widgets would be for about 60–80 units of blue widgets. If you are ordering the blue widgets from a wholesale company, then you might have to round up to the nearest 12 or number of widgets in a case.

If you are using a thrifting or clearance retail arbitrage model, you might not be able to replenish items once sold. So, you would be looking to refine an area of specialty where you have a good idea of what items are in high demand and hard to find. Then you would look to buy a wide variety of items in the areas in which you specialize.

While you're buying your items, you want to stay focused on finding inventory that sells at a steady rate. If you are an Amazon seller, then you probably know that any inventory you hold longer than six months gets charged a whopping $11–22 a square foot in August and February. So there is a set cost to hold your inventory, even if it isn't in your home.

If you store inventory in your home or in your warehouse, there is a cost for the space it takes up. Plus, there is the mental drain you get from seeing that inventory day after day and knowing it will likely be there for months to come.

However, stale inventory costs you the most in lost opportunity. When you have a backlog of stale inventory, you tend to have capital—that could be used to buy items that you could turn several times—tied up for long periods of time. The lost income opportunity of buying inventory that would have a faster turn rate compounds the amount that stale inventory costs you each month.

For example:

You have 100 small widgets that cost you $10 that you expect to profit an incredible $30 each for a total of $3,000 profit. It takes you 6 months to sell through the widgets, so no long-term storage fees are accrued.

Your profit about $3,000 off of your $1,000 investment. You now have $4,000 (original investment + $3,000 profit).

Instead, you buy only 20 of those small widgets. You sell those in just over a month for a profit of $600.

You take the remaining $800 ($1,000 investment minus $200 in small widgets) and purchase several other widgets that give you only a profit of 50%. You buy only a month or less of inventory. At the end of the first month, you have an additional $400 in profit.

You now have doubled your money (profits + your original investment) ($600 + $400 + $1,000). You find only items with a 50% return for the remaining 5 months.

Month 2 – (2,000 + 1,000) = $3,000

Month 3 – (3,000 + 1,500) = $4,500

Month 4 – (4,500 + 2,250) = $6,750

Month 5 – (6,750 + 3375) = $10,125

Month 6 – (10,125 + 5062) = $15,187

At the end of the 6 months you now have $15,187. That is more than $11,000 more than if you had bought all of the higher profit widgets.

Now, these numbers are oversimplified and these numbers do not take into account that there are some additional expenses with turning inventory more times (time to source, prep, etc.). However, the point is to demonstrate that there is a cost for lost opportunity in over buying, even if the item you are holding is selling at a higher margin.

There are people who have entire businesses based on buying things and holding them. Usually, these buyers focus on discontinued or limited edition items. This can be a great way to charge a hefty premium for items. However, you have to have enough capital to hold the item until it becomes rare enough to get the best price.

While those who buy and hold don't turn their inventory as many times, they can focus on processing a smaller amount of inventory for greater profit per item.

Margin

The next thing that you need to understand to keep your business healthy is your margins. We cannot overemphasize the importance of knowing exactly how much you profit off an item. Expenses can add up quickly, and it is easier than one would think to be losing money selling online or even in a brick and mortar store and not realize it. Having buying habits that focus on knowing which items are going to make you the most money is crucial for long-term success.

Profit vs. Sales

When you look at how much you're going to "make" off of an item, you want to take the amount that you're going to receive from the customer and subtract your costs. Say you have an item that you're going to get $20 from the customer for, and it costs you $10 to purchase the item. If it costs you another $2 for the packaging materials, now the cost is at $12. Let's say you have to ship it to the customer— that will cost you another $3, so you're now at $15. It might at first glance look like you would've made $10 on that sale, but when you include some of the other costs, you realize you're making less. While your gross sales on this item are $20, your net profit is only $5.

One of the things that I see people who are new to business do that can lead them into trouble is assuming they are making money because they have sales. Just because you're having sales does not necessarily mean that you're making money. In the example above, if shipping had been $10 instead of $3, then your net profit would be a loss of $2.

To be profitable, you need to make sure that you're including all of the costs involved in selling an item. Shipping the item to you, shipping to the customer, and labor in prepping and packing the item are all calculated. While you're in that first milestone, you can get away with having a general idea of profit. You are just learning, and there will be unexpected expenses. However, as you grow from $5,000 to $20,000 a month, it becomes increasingly more important that you manage your margins well.

In addition to understanding your turn rate and margins, invest in some good books about business. You can find a lot more information on these concepts by reading business books or by simply Googling the terms you want to learn about more in depth. Here are a couple of terms you will want to research and understand for this milestone:

- Gross Sales
- Gross Net
- Profit
- Return on Investment
- Net Profit

You can also check out the resources page for this book at www.BestFromTheNest.com/UNLIKELY-Resources to find a list of books that I recommend to entrepreneurs.

Pricing is, in general, is a function of supply and demand.

The more products you carry with a high demand but short supply (hard to find), the more you can charge for items. If you're interested in learning more about how supply and demand works, I highly recommend a video called *Supply & Dance* by We the Economy.

Step 3
Foundation building.

At this milestone, even if you're intent is to maintain your sales and not grow, you are a real business. As such, it is very important that you're taking care of the following items if you haven't done so already.

Business basics:
- Filing a business entity if needed
- Becoming a registered business owner and filing for any necessary tax licenses
- Opening a separate bank account
- Obtaining business liability insurance
- Consulting with an accountant
- Having a weekly cash flow
- Having an inventory buying plan for each month
- Understanding the difference between an employee and contractor to the IRS

You should also be looking at paying yourself; especially if you are an LLC or an S-corp, you're going to want to talk to your accountant about paying yourself a salary.

Creating systems is something that has been integral in

having our business grow the way that it has. Even if it's just you working your business, at this point you should be writing down exactly how you do things. Imagine if you were to get sick, if you want to go on vacation, if there were a family emergency—you should start training someone who could fill in for you in an emergency.

We sell toys primarily. A couple of years ago, during the fourth quarter, I got very ill and had to be hospitalized. You would think that our income would've gone down that year for that month. However, year over year that month we did 50% more in gross sales. The reason was that I had systems in place. When an emergency happened, other people were able to step in and help us.

Amazon Specifics for Milestone 1

If you are growing a business on Amazon, and you plan to continue selling on this marketplace, I recommend you branch out and learn the following so that you can expand that business:

- How to create listings
- Understanding Parent Child Variations
- Keywords and organic search
- Amazon-sponsored product ads
- Reports area (especially inventory health, customer concessions, and sales and traffic by ASIN)
- Prohibited, restricted, and gated items
- Amazon policies on perishable items and item prep
- Order defect rate

Craigslist Specifics for Milestone 1

If you're selling on Craigslist, you want to make sure that you understand the Craigslist terms of service. Also, get with your accountant to make sure that you're recording all of your cash transactions and that you're paying the proper amount of taxes.

eBay Specifics for Milestone 1

If you're on eBay, you want to make sure that you understand the following terms:

- Top Rated Seller Program
- Power Seller Requirements
- Order Defects
- Feedback Policies
- Fast N Free Shipping
- Global Shipping Program
- Return Policies
- Cassini

Local Service Specifics for Milestone 1

If you're offering a local service, things that you should be looking at include any licenses that are required. These items should have been done in milestone 1, but if you haven't done so, do that today.

Make sure that your taxing correctly for the service, and if you haven't done that already, make sure that you pay any back taxes before the filings and fees become even greater.

Make sure you have business insurance for when you're driving. Your personal auto insurance might not cover you in an accident that was related to your business.

Make sure you have a good business insurance policy and remember, it is your responsibility to do the research. There is information on the resources page for this book on how to find out more about some of those items.

Step 4
Increasing revenue.

To increase revenue, you're going to be looking to create systems for scaling. Look for low-cost ways to increase revenue. When we were trying to scale our Amazon business, what we would do is set a weekly inventory goal. So if our goal was to send in $1,000 in good inventory to Amazon, we would do whatever it took, outside of stealing, to find the goal amount in inventory. If we didn't have enough capital to purchase items at retail stores, we would go back to finding used books. Even today we use a combination of sourcing methods to ensure we are always sending in quality inventory to Amazon.

We do the same with our eBay business as well. We set a plan and try new methods of sourcing inventory so that we can continue to rely on the income from our eBay sales.

For those selling on Amazon, at milestone 2 I recommend looking at new sourcing techniques. There is a lot of information already out there on most of these techniques, so they are easy to learn. Techniques that work well in this milestone are used books, retail arbitrage, and online arbitrage. Wholesale can be done at this milestone with caution. Remember that lead times for wholesale are longer, and sometimes you might do better with arbitrage or books to get higher margins at this stage.

I would not recommend importing or private labeling. There is a lot of risk and liability involved, and you might not have the capital to support the production or transit times of your inventory.

For those growing on Craigslist, you would be looking at adding more areas of expertise for buying. You could also create a team of buyers who would go out and buy inventory for you. You could also outsource the cleaning and listing of your inventory.

Another option could also be finding a local commercial space where you could have your goods available for sale, and the customers could come in at their leisure.

For local services, to increase revenue you could look at add-on services, up-sells, gathering testimonials, and raising prices for new customers.

CHAPTER SEVEN:
MILESTONE 3

Getting to milestone 3 can be exciting and a little daunting. If you started like us, with nothing, and have grown your business to this size, it can be kind of like losing a lot of weight very quickly. When you look in the mirror you still see that person that you used to be, even though who you have become has changed dramatically. You are a real business owner. You are not just somebody in your living room anymore. You are not somebody who has just started with nothing. You are a business owner, a successful business owner.

At this stage, it is very important you have people in your life that can give you objective advice about your business. You want to seek out people who have achieved the results you are looking for and partner with them. Whether it be an accountability partner, mentor, or coach, having someone who will help keep you in consistent action will make a dramatic difference in the profitability of your company.

It was at milestone 3 that I met one of my mentors, Pat Pepe. She was able to see me and my business in a way that I could not. Also, since she had the experience I didn't have, she was able to be a reliable sounding board for me. I was able to come to her for advice and know that I was getting solid feedback. She gave me room to make mistakes and learn on my own, but gave me the courage to swing for the fences and take on things I might never have dared without her advice.

When looking for a mentor, you want someone who is, at their core, a person that loves to teach and share. To find this person you will probably have to go outside of your comfort zone, but I can tell you it is very worthwhile. Pat has also introduced me to many other business owners whom I admire and can rely on for very honest advice.

At this point, you have to face some important decisions regarding what direction you want to take your business. Some people choose to grow their business, wanting to build teams, find warehouse space, and create multiple income streams. Some people want to focus on maximizing their profits and making sure that they're getting the best possible value out of the income that their business is providing them. In this milestone, we'll be going over both situations.

Remember this is your business, and you know your business better than anyone else. If the ideas don't apply to you or will not get you where you want to ultimately go, then don't use them. I do, however, suggest that regardless of whether you use the tips that I've laid out below, that you take the time to make sure that you learn about your business and that you create a long-term plan so that you can make sure that you get the desired results.

Step 1
Goal setting.

In milestone 2, we set a one-year goal or two-year goal. At this point, I feel strongly that you should have not only a one- and two-year goal but a three- and five-year goal. You should also take time to consider your exit strategy. Do you want to ultimately sell this business? Is this something that you're going to do as long as it's profitable, or is this something that you plan to do for a short period of time?

Having those decisions made now will help you move your business in the right direction. If you want to sell your business ultimately, there's going to be different tasks that you're going to want to do to make sure your business will be sellable. Also, you will have different considerations on how you structure other income streams. If you're not looking to sell your business, if you're looking to grow and make this a long-term career, then there also are different strategies that you're going to want to take.

Make sure that you talk with your accountant or attorney to make sure that your long-term plans and the actions that you take today both line up together. Redo the activity from milestone 1 in the goal-setting section to make sure that you have goals set for both the short and long term.

Step 2
Understanding your business.

At this stage in your business, you have probably become masterful at quite a few things. However, there are always areas to improve on. Refining and mastering the skills that you need in order to make your business profitable, to make sure that your inventory is consistently turning, and that your margins stay at a profitable level is a result of not only the actions you take but also the knowledge that you gain as you read books, blogs, and Facebook posts.

One of the important things in refining and mastering the processes in your business is to make sure that you have the right tools. Sometimes to save money, we try to make due with tools that don't work any longer, or we try to work within systems that are antiquated. You could be trying to process inventory in a space that's just really too small, using an inventory system that isn't built to handle the volume you process, or still trying to do it all yourself.

You want to make sure that you're being fiscally responsible, but make sure you also are getting the tools that you need. Moving into a warehouse allowed us to process a lot more inventory a lot quicker without having to increase our staffing levels. By getting the right tools, we were able to increase our profit margins and maximize the staff that we already had on the payroll.

Make sure you set up your environment to win. Make sure that your office is a place that you feel comfortable working in and where you feel productive. Make sure that your warehouse is organized in a way that makes sense. Is the bubble wrap near the prep station? Are the items that need to be shipped out the most often closest to the warehouse door?

If you have a warehouse, or you're going to be stocking a lot of merchandise yourself, make sure that you take the time to read about how to set up your warehouse correctly. Ensure that your shelves are organized so that your staff doesn't waste time trying to find things and that there's a workflow that is clear even to people who are new to your staff.

The last thing to do in refining and mastering the processes for your business is to make sure that you're preparing for the rain. In the movie *Facing the Giants,* there is a portion of the movie where a parable is told of two farmers that ask God to send rain for the fields. The one farmer simply prays, and the second farmer prays and then prepares the field for the rain. The storyteller says that only the second farmer had faith, because he prepared for his prayers to be answered.

Whether or not you believe in God, whether or not you are a person that prays, if you want your business to succeed, you need to prepare for success. You need to prepare for the rain, so that means if you have plans to grow your business to a certain level, you want to make sure that your business is set up to get to that level.

If you want to sell $100,000 a month, the first thing to do is to not add a new sourcing method. The first thing to do is get your processes refined, lean, and streamlined to the point where you can process that much inventory as smoothly and as effectively as possible. That's going to increase the amount of money that goes in your pocket at the end of the day.

As you are growing and understanding your business, you might choose to build teams and to outsource. The first step in hiring people isn't necessarily to post a job position. The first step is going to be to create systems and to create a step-by-step guide for everything that you're going to do and everything that you want somebody else to do. I try to make sure we have text and video directions for all the processes in our business. The exception to this is something that you would outsource to a company, such as accounting or housecleaning. You don't need to write up steps for them because they're going to have their own process.

The second step before you hire somebody is to get self-aware. You need to know your strengths and weaknesses and not just what you think your strengths and weaknesses are. Ask your close friends and people who have worked with you what your strengths are and what items are things that you could work on.

In the area of your strengths, what you know that you love to do and what you're really good at, that's where you want to focus most of your work. Most of your work should be handling managing the business growing and focusing on the things that are your strengths. If you're masterful at finding great inventory, focus on that. If you're masterful at doing the numbers and the spreadsheets, then you should have that be the bulk of your job description.

In the areas that you're weak, rather than trying to become something that you're not, embrace who you are and embrace those weaknesses. Find people that round you out. I am not a very detail-oriented person, so I am horrible in the warehouse. I miss stickers. I prep things the wrong way. I mislabel things. I'm not good in the warehouse, so I don't work in the warehouse, and it's not because the warehouse is beneath me. It's because I'm not good at it. Gabe, my warehouse manager, is much better at it than I am. His strengths are in the area that he works in.

Rochelle is really great at managing the operations and the day-to-day things that need to happen and making sure that all those little details get done while looking at the bigger scope of the big picture. That's not necessarily my strength, but it's her strength, so that's the area that she works in.

Before you hire somebody, first you need to find what areas you're weak in so you know that's where you want to hire people first. You might think that you would be ready to hire somebody at this point, but before you even do that, my recommendation is to identify key values that you want to have in your business. Make sure that you have those values ready to present to whomever you bring into your company, whether they are contractors or employees.

To give you an example of this, I'll tell you what I tell most people when they come to work for us. Working here, integrity is the most important thing. There is nothing I value over integrity, so if you tell me you're going to do something, I expect you to do it or I expect you to tell me as soon as you realize you're not going to be able to do it. I also tell new hires that I consider theft of time as theft and that I expect them when they're on the clock to be actually working and that if they need time off that we will be happy to work with them, but I just need them to be in communication with me.

The second key value that we have is problem-solving. If somebody comes up against a problem, we don't want them to just throw their hands in the air and say, "I can't figure it out." We want them to say, "How can I figure this out? How can I work with this?" and then make sure that they're getting input from the team. So, problem-solving is an important part of being on our team.

Another value we hold is excellence—doing everything with pride and with quality. We also value having fortitude, not giving up, being willing to stand up after a fall, and to keep on moving.

As you make your first hires, you're also going to want a way for your team to keep score. Let them know what specific results you want them to achieve. In order to know that, you have to have done the job that they're going to be doing or have had somebody else do that job so that you know what they should be able to expect.

When we bring somebody into the warehouse, and we ask them to put items in polybags to prep them for Amazon's warehouse, we say, "Here's how we do this process, and we expect you to be able to do at least 50 of these per hour," or, "...at least 100 of these per hour," depending on the complexity of the task. This way they know what their expectations are.

You also want to make sure everyone on your team knows the long-term goals that you have for your business. If you are going to be running this business only for two or three years and then selling it, then you probably are going to want to hire different people than if you were planning to build this business from a small business to a large business over time.

One way that we were able to grow as quickly as we did is because we hired virtual assistants very early on. I have a course on how to hire and train virtual assistants, so I'm not going to go super in-depth here on how to do this. You can find out more about the course in the resources page for this book. Basically, what we did is we hired people in the Philippines, and we were able to provide those people a great job. They work from home. They work in an area when they feel comfortable and on their own schedule without having to leave, and we pay them very well for their region.

We pay people in the Philippines about $3–$6 per hour, and we have them handle everything from data entry to calendaring to graphic design. We've even had them take inbound calls for us. Having a virtual assistant can really reduce a lot of expenses, and you don't have to pay for a computer or a space for them, so it's a really great way to start growing your business so that you can hire locally.

I know that we wouldn't be able to be at the point where we

are able to hire so many people inside the US if we hadn't hired people outside the US first. We could not have been able to support somebody and be able to promise them either part-time or full-time employment. Now we have several employees and many contractors around the globe.

Regarding looking for local help, I love to hire college students. They're ambitious, but they're focused on school. They really need flexibility, and I can provide them that flexibility in their schedule. They can work ten to two on Wednesday and three to five on Thursday. They're innovative, and they're excited to try something new, so I love hiring college students.

Other people that make really great part-time help are people who are recently retired, stay-at-home moms, stay-at-home dads, anybody that just needs a little bit of extra income.

When you're hiring somebody, don't look for somebody that needs a job. Somebody that needs a job most likely is not going to stay, or they could be somebody that needs a job because maybe they're not a very good employee. When you're looking to hire, look for somebody that has strengths that you're looking for. Look for somebody that is willing to work hard and provide something of value to your team.

Make sure that you give them ownership. One of the ways that we do this is that we introduced a profit-sharing program. I also give bonuses quite often for hard work, and I make sure that I tell the people that work for me how wonderful they are and what a great contribution they are to our business and to our lives. Giving people respect for their contribution to the livelihood that you have is important as a business owner.

Step 3
Adding New Streams of Income.

Adding a new stream of income provides stability and security. Each income stream, as we discussed earlier in the book, should be completely independent of the other streams. If you sell on Amazon and Amazon suspends your account, then you can no longer sell on Amazon. However, if you sell on Amazon and eBay, then you have two streams of income. If Amazon suddenly decided they didn't want you to sell on there anymore, then you would still have your eBay income to help support you and your contractors and employees.

Adding a new stream can come in many different ways. You could be selling in a new marketplace. You could create your own e-Commerce website. You could provide consulting to smaller businesses that are looking to grow. You could teach. Some great information on finding new streams of income can be found in the book *Silent Sales Machine* by Jim Cockrum. You can also find out about teaching online through websites like Udemy and Skillshare.com.

The other option is to provide a service. Look at maybe finding an area that you excel at and helping other businesses in your area. If you excel at managing your inventory, then you can offer inventory management assistance. The same numbers that you're doing for your business you can do for somebody else. Help them grow their business, and you can provide an extra additional stream of income for yourself.

Step 4
Foundation building.

As you're growing your business, you want to make sure that not only are you learning more about your industry and about changes that are happening in the marketplaces that you're selling on but also that you have a good understanding of business itself.

One of the ways that I do this is I try to make sure that I read lots of non-fiction books. I try to read up on other people that I want to be like and try to emulate some of the things and characteristics that they have so that I can have some of the success that they have. Find others who do the same thing as you but do it better, offer them something of value, and ask for their advice on your business. Most people are happy to share with others who are eager to learn and eager to work.

Joining a business group can be an amazing way to not only meet other people that you can talk about your business with but also to find new skills and to get new ideas for your business. When I joined the Internet Merchants Association, I was a little bit nervous. I had never really joined a group like that. I wasn't sure if I was really a big enough business to really qualify as being a member, but I found that that camaraderie that I had with my fellow IMA members helped me to grow my business a lot faster. Not only did I have a sounding board from other people in my industry that I could bounce ideas off of, but I was able to help others grow their business, too.

You might find, like I did, that once you start teaching other people how to do things, it helps you clarify things for yourself. It helps you to have better understanding of the bigger picture, so it helps you refine your own processes. Also, when you're teaching somebody to do something, you feel a little bit obligated to do what you're teaching, so it can help you improve your own systems.

Once I started lecturing my coaching clients on the importance of having a working cash flow and knowing their numbers, I found I was better at maintaining that discipline myself. Sometimes being in a position of leadership calls you into action in a way that can be indescribable.

As we did in milestone two, make sure that you read up on taxes and laws. Consult an accountant and an attorney to make sure that you're following all the regulations for your industry. If you're selling on a marketplace, make sure that you're constantly looking at the terms of service and the policies and guidelines to make sure that you're staying in compliance so that your account remains in good standing.

If you still do not have business insurance, and I talk with a surprising number of entrepreneurs at milestone three that do not, get it today. More than likely you will never need it. However, if you do, business insurance protects your home and assets. This is not something that can wait.

If you have employees, you also need to have workers compensation insurance. Check with state laws to see what is required in your city and state.

Step 5
Growing your main income stream.

Usually when people talk about growing their business, the first thing they go to is, "How can I get more inventory?" or "How can I get more sales?" The problem that I have with focusing on sales and inventory is that most of the time they are not focused on the real question, "How can I make my business more profitable?"

A lot of entrepreneurs leave a lot of money on the table buying and selling things that they're not making money on, keeping their staff and themselves very busy, but not making a lot of profit.

It always breaks my heart every year around tax season. Someone will start posting on Facebook groups that they just realized that the last year they didn't make as much money as they thought they did. Even worse, that they lost money when they thought they'd been making money this whole time.

As we talked about in milestone 2, there are two ways to make sure that your business is generating a profit for you and not just generating sales. We talked about inventory turn rate and margins.

We're going to go into a little more depth into inventory turn rate. Inventory turn rate is easy to calculate, but it can be difficult to understand, and the numbers can give you misleading results, especially in seasonal businesses.

To calculate your inventory turn rate, you simply take the cost of goods over the average inventory that you have.

(Cost of Goods Sold)/Average Inventory = Inventory Turn Rate

Let's say on average you have $100,000 in inventory at Amazon at any given point in time, and each year you sell $400,000 in inventory. That would give you a turn rate of four, so that would mean that you turn your inventory four times a year.

$$\$400,000 / \$100,000 = 4$$

Low inventory turn rates can indicate that you have a lot of surplus or stale inventory. Inventory that has been hanging around for a long time is not only eating up storage space but is keeping capital tied up and unable to be used to purchase profitable items. It could also indicate that you could have a bad buying strategy. Maybe you're not buying the right items, or they are not priced competitively.

The dangerous part about a low inventory turn rate is that it can indicate low liquidity, meaning that you don't have access to cash. Your capital is tied up in inventory that you can't expect to be liquid again shortly. Liquid capital is really important as you need cash to grow. Improving your turn rate will allow you to have the cash that you need to grow and sustain your business.

Low inventory turn rate can also mean that your inventory has become obsolete, perhaps a trend that is no longer in style or is now out of date.

High inventory turn rates can indicate that you have good sales and that you're making smart buying decisions. As a result, you'll have liquidity, which means more cash and more options for you to grow and greater ability to take advantage of sales, liquidations, or other investment opportunities that you see. It can also indicate that you've been able to adapt to market changes and that you're able to anticipate upcoming trends.

Remember that an inventory turn rate is just a tool. It's not an exact number, so you want to use inventory turn rate to have a better idea of how inventory is moving through our business. If you have done the calculations, and you find that you have a low inventory turn rate, that doesn't mean that you're a bad business owner. It just means that you have a little bit of work to do in this area.

To deal with turn rate, there are three main strategies. One is to increase sales without increasing inventory, such as offering a sale, clearance, or inventory liquidation. This allows your sales to increase and to sell through the old before purchasing more inventory.

Another strategy is to decrease the amount of inventory that you have without increasing any sales. What that would mean is that it would be time to dispose of inventory. You might say, "Well, I hate to throw away all that good money!" However, sometimes it can be better just to cut your losses, destroy, give away, or liquidate inventory so that you have the freedom to make better buying decisions in the future.

Increasing sales and decreasing inventory is the third option. This will be a combination of the two, where maybe perhaps you put some items on sale or clearance and you liquidate or dispose of another portion of your inventory.

There are some very simple ways that you can improve your inventory turn rate. One of the things that we do that I think has made the biggest impact is that we buy items that have the highest margin first. Then we look at items that have good turn rates that have been consistently selling through, and those get ordered second. We make sure that if we have an item that we could make 80% ROI and another item that we only get 50% ROI, that the item with 80% ROI item is ordered first.

Another way to improve your inventory turn rate is to buy in smaller quantities and to buy more frequently. Yes, you might lose some discounts from buying in bulk or you might have to pay more for shipping to you, but those costs are minimal compared with the cost of getting stuck with stale inventory.

Now, again, I'm a conservative person, and I don't like risk, so this approach doesn't work for all businesses. If you want to go deep into one or two or three lines or buy by the pallet or by the truckload, then I'm probably not the best person to get advice from in this area. Find somebody who's really successful doing that and find out their process.

Of course, you want to make sure that they're making money, but take the pieces of their process that work and apply that to your business.

The second thing that we do to make sure that we get the profit in our pocket instead of just making more work for ourselves is carefully watch our margins. Isolate what products or services that you offer have the highest margins, and focus on that. Most likely you've already heard of the 80/20 rule—that 20% of your products will end up being 80% of your sales. Make an active decision to focus on the products that provide you the greatest profit. Eliminate all the other items, items that might keep you busy but not make you as much money.

Focusing on the products that make you the most money frees up your resources and frees up capital for you to make better investments. It allows you to get focused on items that pay the bills. We did this recently, and we have found that we were further able to streamline our processes. Our entire staff has a reduced workload, and we are making more in profit than when we carried "everything."

Sometimes people get so caught up in wanting to grow their business that it compromises their margins and they lose focus on the long-term gain. Remember, you want to look at what's going to get you to that long-term goal that you set at the beginning of the milestone. If you can keep your margins high, most likely you'll be able to reach those goals quicker than if you compromise and start selling lower margin items and aren't able to have the cash you need in order to grow.

Step 6
Sourcing inventory.

At this point of growth, the next action step will be more individually based on what you do, what niche you sell, and where you sell. I do have some smart starting points. Now is the time that you might want to consider purchasing wholesale, importing, or private-labeling a product.

If you are doing retail arbitrage for sale on Amazon or eBay, instead of purchasing items by yourself, create lists of items, turn those into buy lists, and then have a team go out and purchase those items. Find creative ways to scale your operation and find a unique group of niches that you know well.

You can use virtual assistants to help you manage part of the data entry or the processing and listing the items or services you are selling. They can also help others with other aspect of your business or provide an up-sell opportunity.

Another way to grow your business at this point would be to offer products or services in a new area. Sometimes that can be a new marketplace, a new part of town, or a new subsection of the population.

Make sure you're working with your plan in mind. Use the goal from Step 1 in this milestone to find more detailed sub-goals and map those out. Look at what changes you need to make in your business to get you to the next milestone.

Some examples of questions that you should be looking at are

- How much inventory do you need to send in weekly to hit your next milestone goal?
- How many new customers would you need to add to make sales at a certain profit level?
- How much does each customer cost you?
- How can you get the work done faster while keeping the same level of quality?
- What advertising method is working the best for you and provides the best quality of customers?
- How can you increase margins or become an elite or premium service?

By building teams, focusing on profitability, and becoming hyper-focused on creating systems that are duplicable, you can scale your business faster and pass off work to others so that you can add new streams of income or spend time with family and friends.

CHAPTER EIGHT:
MILESTONE 4

At milestone 4 you've reached something that many business owners can only dream of—surpassing the half million dollar mark in yearly sales. When we passed that mark, for us, it still felt like we hadn't made it yet. In fact, there was a running joke in our office that one day we would be a real business. This joke took on such a life of its own that for Christmas my operations manager, Rochelle, gave me a framed photo of us. In the frame was some of the memorable moments of the year with the heading over the top that said, "We're A Real Business."

This milestone was the first time that I realized that I was at choice. We could create anything. We now had the experience of starting multiple businesses. We started to create more around our passions. You start to see opportunity everywhere. You realize that you can do whatever it is that you want for your business. Do you want to have your business to have an altruistic focus? Do you want to monetize something that you love?

You are no longer limited to just one or two ways of making money. You now have the connections and skills that you need to grow your business. Anything is possible.

The key to growing at this stage is surrounding yourself with strong people that support you. Have a network of people that you can look up to and who can provide an objective, honest point of view for your business. Continue to strive for excellence in everything you do.

Your business has achieved a success level that is not attained by very many people, so you should be very proud of what you have accomplished so far. When I originally designed the milestones, I had a milestone 5 at 100 thousand dollars in gross sales. However, at that amount of annual sales per year, you really should be consulting with companies and consultants that have the expertise to give you the right tools individualized for your business.

What I can do for milestone 4 is I can give you a starting place to look for where you should be growing and where you should be refining your business. If the revenue that you are bringing in now is enough for you to sustain your life and provide for your family the way that you need, one option is to focus on how you can replace a portion of what you do in your business and have other people do it so that you can have more time free to spend your family and friends.

If you are still looking to grow, you will still need to replace yourself in your other streams to allow you the time and flexibility to create new income streams or pursue investments.

Step 1
Re-examine your goals.

Look at the milestone 2 goal setting practice and also look for best- and worst-case scenarios. Be looking at exit strategies and how long you intend to continue running your business. Sometimes when you're looking at your goals, you have to be willing to go backward. At milestone 4 we had to choose to take a conscious step back and regroup so that we could address some processes that were, to be frank, very broken.

Don't let your business trap you. Sometimes it's better to temporarily or permanently slow or shrink your business so that you can have the lifestyle that you want to have long term. Take an honest inventory of what is working, what is not working, and what, in your business, could be working better to get you to your personal goals. Remember to work backward and get immediate action plans. Set out the action plans for one-week, one-month, three-months, six-months, and one-year results.

Step 2
Understanding your business.

We've talked in depth about increasing your margins and watching your inventory turn rate, and you now know that you want to be refining in your business for what makes you a possible profit. Make your business as streamlined as possible. The key, really, at this point in business is that you need to be able to have some freedom. You've put your blood, sweat, and tears into this business, and if you haven't already, it's time to start thinking about how you can enjoy some of the success that you have. If you're like me and you just have a driven personality, you love to create, you love to help others, and you love to start new things, then continue doing that. Help others grow their businesses, and through the service of others you'll find even more prosperity than you're already having.

If you're somebody that you've reached the level of income that you want, then now it's time to start looking at what the next step is for you. Is this a business that you want to have that you work on the side on a limited basis to keep providing your income, or is this something that you are looking to sell and retire? Depending on your age and where you are in your life, you want to make sure that you're heading in the right direction for you to attain your long-term goals.

The only way to have that freedom to either create new businesses or to allow yourself to maybe have some personal time is to hire and train a great team. This team will need to be able to handle things while you're away or while you're creating new things.

We started on Craigslist. Then we moved to eBay, and we got eBay really under control. Then we had contractors take over almost all of our eBay business.

We then added our Amazon stream of business, and I've passed that off to people on my team. Then we started doing course work in consulting. As we mastered it, I added new people to my team, and we made sure that everybody was cross trained.

I have found that letting go of control is the hardest part for many entrepreneurs. Many of us live in fear that if we aren't there to control everything, it will all fall apart. Some fear that there is no one that we can trust something so important to. Perhaps having been burnt one time to many, they hold onto their business with an iron grip, usually micromanaging the capable people on their team until they leave to work for someone who will respect them enough to grant them some level of trust.

I found people that were able to do portions of my business that I didn't think could be outsourced before. We could now outsource these areas because I had built a foundation of great systems, systems that work, and people that work really well together. If you haven't done that at this point, now would be a good time to do that. The most important things when you're hiring somebody or choosing whether or not you want to continue employing somebody are trust and delegation. You have to empower people to do things, and you need to let them do them—and that means letting people make mistakes.

Trust takes time to build. So hire someone, pay them well, and let them do their job. Once you feel like you have the right person, book a three-week vacation. Why? If you don't have something in the future that will force you to give them enough control to handle things while you are away for a couple of weeks, it is easy to end up still doing everything.

Use the time before your trip to make sure you have gone through exactly what needs to be done from day to day. Take a couple days off as a trial. Then enjoy your trip. When you come back, and you have some perspective, see how much control you REALLY want back.

Now that you have had a chance to prove to yourself that your team is fine without you (I find that sometimes I actually slow my team down), you can create the next chapter of your life and your business from a place of freedom and not be trapped in what you did previously.

Use times of prosperity to save for leaner times. Retaining income is something you should be talking about with your accountant. Our next goal is to pay off our house so that even if something changes with our business we are still better off than when we started.

CHAPTER NINE:
SUMMARY

I truly hope that this book has been of help to you, your business, and your team. Building a business can be scary and isolating. When people would marvel at what I had built, I almost felt like a fraud. If they knew how I was holding everything together with duck tape and twine, they wouldn't have had that same admiration for me.

With some time and some insight from great mentors like Pat Pepe and my business coach, Andrea Swenson-Parker, I now see that there was nothing wrong with where I was. We were just a growing business.

There is no point in time that your GPS will go off and let you know that "you have arrived," in your business. Like I have grown as a mother as my children grow, similarly, you will grow into the role of business owner as your business develops.

Take your time. Like childhood, the first years of your

business will hold some of your fondest memories. Some of our favorite stories are from when times were the hardest.

Don't skip steps or take shortcuts. Remember, "all magic comes with a price." If someone has the secret to make your business net you two million dollars this month, they probably would be charging you a lot more than $4,000.

If you enjoyed this book, or even if you didn't, please let me know by shooting me an email at excellence@robynsnest.co. If you see me at an event, say hi and feel free to ask lots of questions. Usually I travel with at least one member from our team, so ask him or her lots of questions, too.

Best of luck in your business and on creating a living.

Appendix

Break Out of Goal Tables

The table for the goal setting section are generalized, and the numbers are rounded. The reason for this depends on your average selling price of your items your actual return will vary. Also, if you send $1000 of inventory into Amazon, not all of that $1000 will sell in the first 30 days. When working with coaching clients, I recommend that if they want to have $10,000 a month in gross sales that they send in $12,000 in inventory a month. This is to account for items that don't sell at the anticipated price or sell slower than anticipated.

Here is the original table from the book:

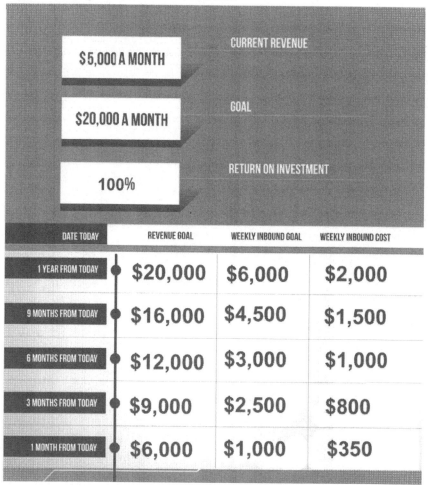

$5,000 A MONTH	CURRENT REVENUE
$20,000 A MONTH	GOAL
100%	RETURN ON INVESTMENT

DATE TODAY	REVENUE GOAL	WEEKLY INBOUND GOAL	WEEKLY INBOUND COST
1 YEAR FROM TODAY	$20,000	$6,000	$2,000
9 MONTHS FROM TODAY	$16,000	$4,500	$1,500
6 MONTHS FROM TODAY	$12,000	$3,000	$1,000
3 MONTHS FROM TODAY	$9,000	$2,500	$800
1 MONTH FROM TODAY	$6,000	$1,000	$350

If you were to look at a table with a lower ROI, the table would change slightly. You would have to spend more weekly to get the same amount of gross sales. However, you would net less for every dollar spent. Here is a table of the same goal markers for 50% ROI:

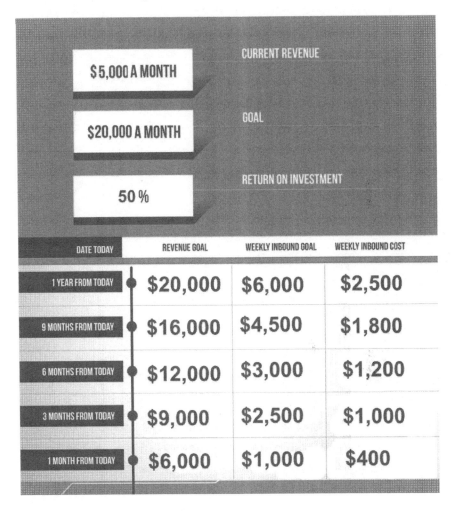

	CURRENT REVENUE
$5,000 A MONTH	
$20,000 A MONTH	GOAL
50%	RETURN ON INVESTMENT

DATE TODAY	REVENUE GOAL	WEEKLY INBOUND GOAL	WEEKLY INBOUND COST
1 YEAR FROM TODAY	$20,000	$6,000	$2,500
9 MONTHS FROM TODAY	$16,000	$4,500	$1,800
6 MONTHS FROM TODAY	$12,000	$3,000	$1,200
3 MONTHS FROM TODAY	$9,000	$2,500	$1,000
1 MONTH FROM TODAY	$6,000	$1,000	$400

Usually, items with a lower ROI are easier to find. However, you will profit much less. For example, on the one month from today goal you need to spend $350 at 100% ROI and $400 at 50% ROI. However, you would profit close to $350 at 100% ROI and only $200 at 50% ROI. So you have to have much more capital and process much more inventory to have the same amount of profit at a lower percentage of return.

	Inbound at 50% ROI	Profit at 50% ROI	Inbound at 100% ROI	Profit at 50% ROI
Weekly Spending Goal	$400.00	$200.00	$350.00	$350.00

So while it is tempting to lower your standards for sourcing to a lower percentage, you have to be aware of the extra amount of work it will take to process items to get the same results.

Also, the lower your margin, the more carefully you have to monitor your expenses. Things like dimensional weight, labor, prep materials, etc. can quickly erode all of your profit. You must make sure that you are calculating your profit after all costs and Amazon fees on every item.

The best way to make sure that you don't make money selling on Amazon or Ebay is to guess on the fees that they charge. Even if you are highly skilled at mathematics, you will need the calculators to correctly determine the amount of profit on each item.

The idea behind these tables isn't to provide a precise mathematical guide. That would be nearly impossible as there are many variables that come into play like inventory turn rate, average selling price, referral fees, etc. The point is to give you a place to start to take action in your business.

Remember it is important to be able to tell whether or not you are winning, this table gives you a way to monitor and pace your actions. To help you stay on track for you goals.

The other purpose of the tables is to provide a reality check. I sometimes will see someone who wants to make $10,000 a month net on Amazon by the end of the year. That is possible with the right amount of capital and hard work. When I break out the goal for them with the actions, they need to take today it helps them to see if their goal is doable within their current circumstances. Breaking your goal down into actions that need to be taken immediately gives you an idea of whether your goal is based in reality or just a hope or a wish.

I am sure that someone will point out that the math on the tables is not completely accurate, and they will be right. The numbers are simplified and rounded. The math isn't the point; the idea is to get to you take action today.

I have provided a couple of blank tables for you to fill out for where you are in your business today.

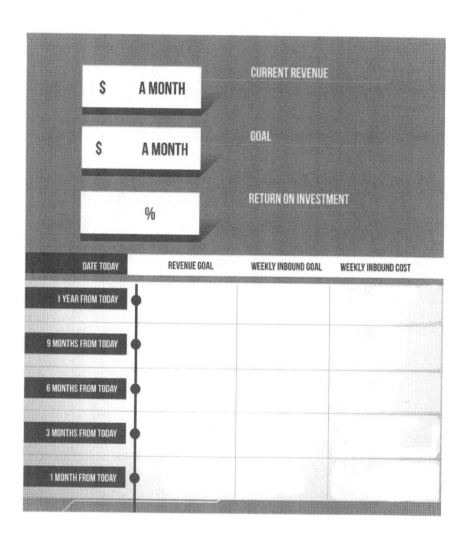

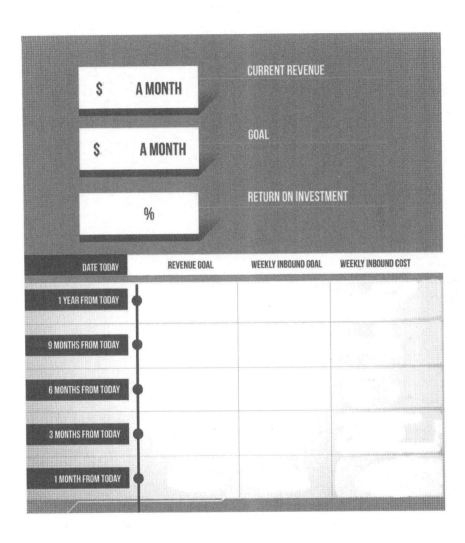

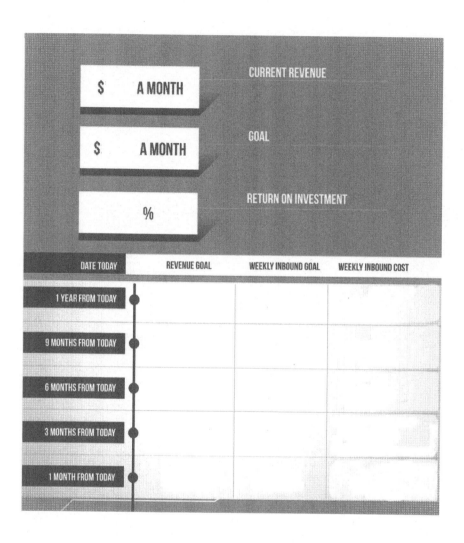

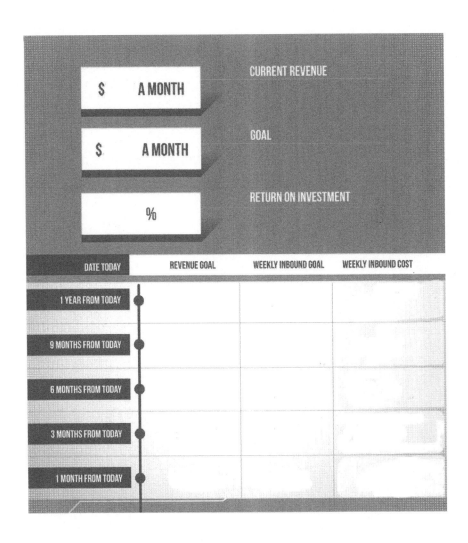

Robyn Johnson

NOTES:

NOTES:

NOTES:

Made in the USA
Middletown, DE
03 November 2015